ELON MUSK

BY SARA GREEN

BELLWETHER MEDIA • MINNEAPOLIS, MN

Jump into the cockpit and take flight with Pilot books. Your journey will take you on high-energy adventures as you learn about all that is wild, weird, fascinating, and fun!

This edition first published in 2015 by Bellwether Media, Inc.

No part of this publication may be reproduced in whole or in part without written permission of the publisher. For information regarding permission, write to Bellwether Media, Inc., Attention: Permissions Department, 5357 Penn Avenue South, Minneapolis, MN 55419.

Library of Congress Cataloging-in-Publication Data

Green, Sara, 1964- author.
 Elon Musk / by Sara Green.
    pages cm. – (Pilot: Tech Icons)
 Summary: "Engaging images accompany information about Elon Musk. The combination of high-interest subject matter and narrative text is intended for students in grades 3 through 7"– Provided by publisher.
 Audience: Ages 7-12.
 Includes bibliographical references and index.
 ISBN 978-1-60014-988-7 (hardcover : alk. paper)
 1. Musk, Elon. 2. Businesspeople–United States–Biography. 3. Businesspeople–South Africa–Biography. 4. Internet industry–Juvenile literature. 5. PayPal (Firm)–Juvenile literature. 6. Clean energy industries–Juvenile literature. I. Title.
 HC102.5.M87G74 2014
 332.1'78–dc23
 [B]
                         2014008253

Printed in the United States of America, North Mankato, MN.

TABLE OF CONTENTS

CHAPTER 1

WHO IS ELON MUSK?

Elon Musk is on a quest to save Earth. This **entrepreneur** first gained success with the Internet. He **co-founded** several companies, including PayPal. Now he dedicates his time to **sustainable energy** and space travel. He co-founded SpaceX, a company that makes rockets. He also designs electric cars at Tesla Motors. By the time Elon was in his late 20s, he was a multimillionaire. Today, Elon is worth more than $11 billion.

Elon was born in Pretoria, South Africa, on June 28, 1971. His mother, Maye, was a **dietitian** and a fashion model. His father, Errol, was an engineer. Elon is the oldest of three children. He has a brother named Kimbal and a sister named Tosca. When Elon was 8, his parents separated. Elon split his time between their houses. Both encouraged him to explore his interests and try new things.

ICON BIO

Name: Elon Reeve Musk

Birthday: June 28, 1971

Hometown: Pretoria, South Africa

Marital status: Married to Talulah Riley since 2010

Children: One set of twins and one set of triplets, all boys

Hobbies/ Interests: Producing movies, researching space and Mars, sports cars

Elon was a bright, creative child. Reading was a favorite pastime. He often read science fiction. Outer space fascinated Elon. But he also had a great memory for facts. He once read an entire set of **encyclopedias**! Elon was one of the youngest kids in his class. He was also small for his age. Sometimes other kids bullied him. When Elon felt lonely, he found comfort in books and computers.

Elon was interested in computers from a young age. He taught himself how to program a computer when he was 10 years old. When he was 12, Elon created a space computer game called Blastar. He sold it to a computer magazine for $500. Around this time, Elon decided he would live in the United States someday. He knew it was a place where people made their dreams come true.

CHAPTER 2
BIG DREAMS

In 1989, at age 17, Elon graduated from Pretoria Boys High School. He moved to Saskatchewan, Canada, where he lived with his grandparents for a short time. He then moved to Ontario, Canada, to attend Queen's University. In 1992, Elon changed schools. He attended the University of Pennsylvania in Philadelphia. There, he thought a lot about the future. He believed three things would affect humans the most. These were the Internet, sustainable energy, and **colonizing** other planets. Elon decided to focus on these areas.

In 1995, Elon graduated from college with degrees in **economics** and physics. He moved to California to study for a PhD in physics at Stanford University. However, Elon was more excited about the Internet than getting another degree. After only two days, Elon left the university. Instead, he started an online **software** company called Zip2. It helped newspapers post maps and city guides on the Internet.

"If something is important enough, even if the odds are against you, you should still do it."

— Elon Musk

9

In 1999, Elon sold Zip2 for $307 mi
computer company called Compaq. At
Elon was a millionaire! He used money
sale to start an online bank called X.com
members, Elon gave $20 to anyone who
online account. He gave $10 to members
referral. In just a few months, the compa
100,000 customers.

Soon, Elon bought another online banking company called Confinity. It included an online payment service called PayPal. Elon combined Confinity with X.com. In 2001, he renamed the entire company PayPal. It quickly became the most popular way to pay online. In 2002, Elon sold PayPal to eBay, an online auction web site, for $1.5 billion. Now he had money to focus on sustainable energy and space travel.

CHAPTER 3

SPACEX

Elon has always had a strong passion for space. In 2002, he founded a private space transport company in California. He named it Space Exploration Technologies Corporation, or SpaceX. It develops rockets and spacecraft for space travel. Elon is the company's **CEO** and Chief Designer. His goal is to make space travel affordable. To do this, he designs cheaper spacecraft. They include rockets that can be used again.

Elon made history in 2008. That year, SpaceX launched the *Falcon 1* rocket into orbit. This was the first time a private company launched a rocket into space! SpaceX has since launched two other vehicles. They are the *Falcon 9* rocket and the *Dragon* spacecraft. SpaceX is also working on a more powerful rocket called *Falcon Heavy*. It will be able to carry 117,000 pounds (53,000 kilograms) into Earth's orbit and perhaps beyond.

STAR WARS NAMESAKES

The Falcon rockets are named after the *Millennium Falcon*, a spacecraft from the *Star Wars* movies.

"I think human exploration of space is very important. Certainly, from a survival standpoint, the probability of living longer is much greater if we're on more than one planet."

— Elon Musk

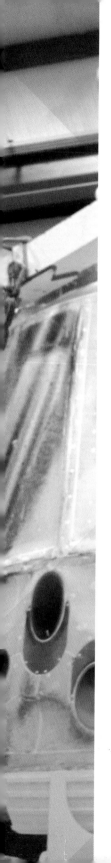

Since 2008, SpaceX has had several successful launches. Many more launches are planned. Rockets are used to bring **satellites** into orbit around Earth. The *Dragon* spacecraft carries cargo to space. It does this without any humans on board. In 2012, *Dragon* delivered supplies to the International Space Station (ISS). Then it returned safely to Earth. *Dragon* was the first **commercial** spacecraft to complete this task.

Elon wants to make space travel as affordable as air travel. Today, SpaceX is working with **NASA** to develop a passenger ship called *DragonRider*. At first, it will carry people into orbit or to the ISS. In time, Elon plans to use these shuttles to colonize other planets. He has his sights set on Mars. Elon knows this will be a challenge. But if he has his way, he will live on Mars someday!

REAL-LIFE IRON MAN

The Tony Stark character in the *Iron Man* movies is based on Elon. Part of *Iron Man II* was filmed in the SpaceX factory. Elon also appears briefly in the movie.

CHAPTER 4
CLEAN ENERGY

Elon dreams of a future when cars will not run on gasoline. In 2004, he **invested** more than $6 million in Tesla Motors in Palo Alto, California. This company designs and makes electric cars. Unlike gasoline-powered cars, electric cars have no **emissions**. They add less **pollution** to the air. Elon quickly became Tesla's CEO and head designer. He has since led the company to great success. Teslas are in high demand!

Elon promotes clean energy in other companies, too. He is the chairman of SolarCity. This company provides solar energy to homes and businesses across the United States. SolarCity also makes **charging stations** for electric cars. In August 2013, Elon described a new idea. It was a train called the Hyperloop. Passengers will ride in pods through tubes at speeds greater than 700 miles (1,127 kilometers) per hour. This is faster than flying in an airplane! Elon hopes to have the Hyperloop built by 2023.

AN AWARD-WINNING CAR
The Tesla Model S was named *Motor Trend* magazine's Car of the Year in 2013.

CHAPTER 5

SUCCESS, TODAY AND TOMORROW

Elon's ideas and leadership have brought him great success and many awards. In 2010, *Time* magazine listed him as one of the world's most influential people. That year, he was also named a "Living Legend in **Aviation**." In 2013, *Fortune* magazine named him Businessperson of the Year.

Elon believes in giving back to others. In 2001, he started the Musk **Foundation**. It helps fund science education and children's health. It also supports research on space exploration and clean energy. This includes running a Mars research station in southern Utah. Visitors can explore a Mars-like landscape. They experience what life might be like on the planet.

In 2012, Elon signed the Giving Pledge. He promised to give away at least half of his wealth to charities over his lifetime. Long into the future, Elon's fortune will help this world and beyond.

RESUME

Education

1992-1995: University of Pennsylvania (Philadelphia, Pennsylvania)
1990-1992: Queen's University (Kingston, Ontario, Canada)
1984-1988: Pretoria Boys High School (Pretoria, South Africa)

Work Experience

2008-present: CEO of Tesla Motors
2006-present: Chairman of SolarCity
2004-present: Chairman/Product Architect at Tesla Motors
2002-present: CEO and Chief Designer of SpaceX
2001: Formed PayPal
1999: Founded X.com, an online payment service
1995: Founded Zip2, an online software service

Community Service/Philanthropy

2012: Donated $1,000,000 to Doctors Without Borders
2011: Donated $250,000 to Soma, Japan, for solar power project
2010: Donated solar power system to Gulf Coast community hit by Hurricane Katrina

LIFE TIMELINE

June 28, 1971:
Born in Pretoria, South Africa

1983:
Creates and sells a videogame called Blastar to a computer magazine

1989:
Graduates from high school and moves to Saskatchewan, Canada

1990:
Moves to Ontario, Canada, to attend Queen's University

1992:
Moves to Philadelphia, Pennsylvania, to attend the University of Pennsylvania

March 2000:
Merges X.com with Confinity

1995:
Moves to California and starts Zip2

March 1999:
Co-founds X.com

PayPal

June 2001:
X.com is renamed PayPal

2006:
Becomes Chairman of SolarCity

October 2002:
Sells PayPal to eBay for $1.5 billion

2008:
SpaceX gets a $1.6 billion contract to make flights to the International Space Station for NASA

June 2002:
Founds Space Exploration Technologies Corporation (SpaceX)

April 2004:
Invests in Tesla Motors

May 2012:
SpaceX becomes the first private company to dock with the International Space Station

TESLA

SPACEX

GLOSSARY

aviation—the business of flying aircraft

CEO—Chief Executive Officer; the CEO is the highest-ranking person in a company.

charging stations—places that supply electricity for electric cars

co-founded—founded a company with one or more other people

colonizing—sending a group of settlers to a place to live there

commercial—designed mainly for profit

dietitian—an expert on diet and nutrition

economics—a science that studies the production and sales of goods and services

emissions—dangerous fumes

encyclopedias—a set of books arranged alphabetically that gives information

entrepreneur—a person who starts businesses

foundation—an organization that provides funds to other charitable organizations

invested—put money into a business or idea

NASA—the National Aeronautics and Space Administration

pollution—substances that make an area dirty or unusable

referral—a person who uses a service recommended by another person

satellites—machines that are sent to space and move around the moon, sun, Earth, or other planets

software—a program that tells a computer what to do

sustainable energy—energy that does not completely use up or destroy the source of energy

TO LEARN MORE

AT THE LIBRARY

Hunter, Nick. *How Electric and Hybrid Cars Work*. New York, N.Y.: Gareth Stevens Publishing, 2014.

McMahon, Peter. *Space Tourism*. Tonawanda, N.Y.: Kids Can Press Ltd., 2011.

Rusch, Elizabeth. *The Mighty Mars Rovers: The Incredible Adventures of Spirit and Opportunity*. Boston, Mass.: Houghton Mifflin Books for Children, 2012.

ON THE WEB

Learning more about Elon Musk is as easy as 1, 2, 3.

1. Go to www.factsurfer.com.

2. Enter "Elon Musk" into the search box.

3. Click the "Surf" button and you will see a list of related web sites.

With factsurfer.com, finding more information is just a click away.

INDEX

The images in this book are reproduced through the courtesy of: Suntzulynn for LE/ Splash News/ Corbis, front cover (top); Bret Hartman/ Corbis, front cover (bottom), pp. 12-13; Bloomberg/ Getty Images, pp. 4-5, 10-11; Kyodo/ Newscom, pp. 6-7; Robyn Beck/ Newscom, pp. 8-9; Paul Sakuma/ AP Images, p. 11; Duane A. Laverty/ AP Images, pp. 14-15; A.F. Archive/ Alamy, p. 15; Mark Blinch/ Corbis, pp. 16-17; ZUMA/ Alamy, p. 18; 360b, p. 21 (top); Space Exploration Technologies Corporation/ Wikipedia, p. 21 (left); Katherine Welles, p. 21 (right).